Our Catholic Life
A READING AND STUDY GUIDE FOR ADULT FAITH FORMATION

6

✦ COMMANDMENTS ✦

LIVING
THE
COMMANDMENTS

Bill Huebsch

**TWENTY-THIRD
PUBLICATIONS**
twentythirdpublications.com

IMPRIMATUR

+ Most Reverend Joseph R. Binzer
Auxiliary Bishop
Archdiocese of Cincinnati
February 9, 2016

The *Imprimatur* ("Permission to
Publish") is a declaration that a
book or pamphlet is considered
to be free of doctrinal or moral
error. It is not implied that those
who have granted the *Imprimatur*
agree with the contents, opinions,
or statements expressed.

Twenty-Third Publications
1 Montauk Avenue, Suite 200, New London, CT 06320
(860) 437-3012 » (800) 321-0411 » www.twentythirdpublications.com

ISBN: 978-1-62785-174-9
Library of Congress Catalog Card Number: 2016939663
Printed in the U.S.A.

Contents

How to use this study guide in seven small-group sessions

Gather. As people arrive for each session, welcome them warmly and offer them refreshments. You may wish to have sacred music playing to set the tone. If people are new to each other, name tags can help break the ice. When everyone has arrived, gather your group and invite them to open their books to today's material.

Begin with *Lectio divina* prayer. Each session opens with a short and prayerful reflection on a scriptural text that is found in that section of the *Catechism*. Here are the steps:

1. Begin with the Sign of the Cross.

2. Read aloud the Introduction for this session.

3. Call everyone to prayer using these or similar words: *Let us turn our hearts to Christ now and hear the word of the Lord.*

4. Invite a member of the group to proclaim the Scripture we present for you.

5. Invite your group members to share about the text, first in twos and threes if you wish, and then as a whole group. Sharing: *What word or phrase in this reading catches your ear? What is God saying to us in this scriptural text?*

6. Now pray in these or similar words:

   *O God, we know that you are with us and that you behold all we
   are about to do. Now grant that, by the power of the Holy Spirit,
   we might be faithful as we study our faith and charitable in how
   we treat each other. Through Christ, our Lord. Amen.*

Read. Moving around the circle in your group and rotating readers,
read aloud each numbered faith statement. Group members should
note items in the material that strike them as especially important.
Do not read aloud the **We Believe** statements. They are provided as
an enhancement to the text.

Group or personal process. When you come to the process notes,
pause to continue around the circle, discussing as the notes direct.
Use our suggestions as a starting point, and add your own questions,
prayers, or action plans.

Finish. As you conclude this session, call everyone to prayer once
again. Reread the scriptural text we used in the beginning. Then
move around the circle one last time to share: *In light of this reading
and what we have learned today, what has touched you most deeply?
What new insight of faith will you carry away from here? What new
questions about faith have arisen for you? How will today's discussion
work its way into your daily life?* Close your session with the prayer
we provide, or lead a spontaneous prayer in which everyone shares
their own prayer.

Session One

NO STRANGE GODS: *the 1ˢᵗ and 2ⁿᵈ commandments*

....

**BASED ON ARTICLES 2083–2132 AND 2142–2159 OF THE
CATECHISM OF THE CATHOLIC CHURCH. TO READ A SUMMARY OF THIS
SECTION, SEE *CATECHISM* ARTICLES 2133–2141 AND 2160–2167**

Introduction

The first commandment calls us to believe in God, to hope in God, and to love God above all else. Since it rejects or denies the existence of God, atheism is a sin against the first commandment. The second commandment enjoins respect for the Lord's name. The name of the Lord is holy. The second commandment forbids every improper use of God's name. Blasphemy is the use of the name of God, of Jesus Christ, of the Virgin Mary, and of the saints in an offensive way.

Scripture

READER: A reading from the Book of Deuteronomy.

Hear, O Israel: The LORD is our God, the LORD alone. You shall love the LORD your God with all your heart, and with all your soul, and with all your might. Keep these words that I am commanding you today in your heart. Recite them to your children and talk about them when you are at home and when you are away, when you lie down and when you rise. Bind them as a sign on your hand, fix them as an emblem on your forehead, and write them on the doorposts of your house and on your gates. (**DEUTERONOMY 6:4–9**)

READER: The word of the Lord.

ALL: Thanks be to God.

The Lord, your God

[1] God loves us. This simple belief is at the basis of our entire moral code. It is at the basis of what we believe about Jesus Christ and his presence among us: Emmanuel. In response to God's insistent and unconditional love, Jesus taught that we should love God in return, with all our heart, all our soul, all our mind, and all our strength.

[2] In this, Jesus echoed the teaching of our ancestors in the faith. The first commandment reflects this divine love. I am the Lord, your God, it says; I brought you out of Egypt, out of slavery there. I set you free. You are free to be faithful. I have loved you with an everlasting love.

[3] You should never chase after false gods who do not free you, never make a graven image or choose a pathway that does not lead to me. "I am the Lord, your God," the traditional wording said; "thou shalt not have strange gods before me."

[4] Our vocation and destiny is to be with God, who is our Creator and Maker. God calls us home to our own very selves by calling us to the divine heart, for we are made in God's own image. False gods deceive us and lead us away from ourselves, for we are not made in their image.

[5] This first commandment leads us to faith in response to God's powerful presence, to hope in response to God's actions, and to love in response to God's love.

WE BELIEVE

The first commandment calls us to believe in, hope in, and love God above all else. This also calls us to reject false gods, avoid superstition, and cultivate a lively faith.

Faith

[6] We are called to believe in God. We should nourish our faith and reject what is opposed to it. We should not doubt what God has revealed and should pray for insight and deeper faith. Cultivating doubt can lead to spiritual blindness. Nor should we remain ignorant about faith, willingly refusing to study it or to become aware of its depth and beauty.

Hope

[7] We are called to hope in God. We should expect God to bless us and to guide us on the divine pathway with love. Despair is hope's opposite and causes us to give up on God's love, give up on being forgiven yet again, and give up on receiving God's mercy. Presumption is also a danger, because it leads us to think that our own abilities and talents are sufficient or to think we need not repent in order to be forgiven.

Charity

[8] We are called to love God and neighbor. We should avoid indifference to others and especially indifference toward God. We should cultivate gratitude in our hearts as well as excitement for

our faith, avoiding the laziness that makes us think our faith will always be there even if we "take a vacation" from it.

Religious acts

[9] We adore God because God is love, and we submit ourselves to this love in order to allow it to fill our lives. We pray to God in thanksgiving and petition, not because God requires this, but because the Spirit lifts our hearts in prayer. We worship God as the first step in our own journey of dying and rising, turning our hearts to what is holy. We promise God our lives in baptism and confirmation, matrimony and holy orders, and entry into religious life. We may also promise to give alms or to pray.

Religious freedom

[10] Christians are called to be light for the world and to share the Good News of God's love with all men and women throughout all time. Because we believe we fulfill our human destiny only by seeking and acknowledging God, we want everyone to share in this. And yet we also believe it is right and proper to have a sincere respect for different religions which frequently reflect a ray of truth that enlightens all people.

[11] We are called to act with charity toward those who do not share our own beliefs, as article 2104 of the *Catechism* reminds us. All men and women must be free to follow their own convictions, and governments should ensure that freedom.

Group or personal process

- How do the teachings of Jesus echo this commandment and the scriptural texts on which it is based? What did Jesus teach that resembles this?

- Why do we "adore" God? What does it mean to do that? How is it done?

- Pause and consider the ways in which God has touched your life, empowered you, called you, given you gifts, and loved you. How does this cause you to be in awe of God?

PART TWO + ARTICLES 2110-2132 OF THE *CATECHISM*

False gods

[12] There are many kinds of false gods and false expressions of faith. The first commandment forbids them all. First, superstition is belief in magical outcomes as a result of our own actions or prayers. When we believe that some external action of ours can bring about the results we want, we have wandered into superstition.

[13] Second, idolatry is believing in the godliness of material things such as gold and silver. This isn't so much concerned with belief in other gods as in making what is not God into a god in our own minds. It might be money or fame or power or pleasure or ideology or persons or civil government or even religion itself. We have many possible idols, and we must be watchful to honor only God.

[14] Third, we are all curious about what the future will bring, but if we turn to any practice to "unveil" the future, we are failing to put our trust in God and to believe that God will guide us. Some of these practices are common and harmless, such as reading the daily horoscope, consulting astrology, and the like. As long as we do not take them more seriously than we take our belief in God's providence, they remain a hobby. But if we begin to believe in them we are believing in a false god. We call this practice, in fact, "divination," which suggests why we consider it out of step with faith.

[15] This also includes magic or sorcery when it is used to attempt to deal with the occult, whether to help someone or curse them; it is out of step with our faith. This might also include wearing charms or special medals and other items that we believe will bring special blessings. All of these practices contradict the honor, respect, and loving awe that we owe to God alone.

WE BELIEVE

Tempting or testing God by offering him "deals" in exchange for favors violates this commandment.

[16] Fourth, we should never test God. When we make deals with God, offering God our commitment to this or that in exchange for favors, we wander into this area. Or when we enter into risky behavior—saying to God that we want protection and thinking we will believe in God only if the protection materializes—we wander into this area.

[17] Fifth, we should not treat the sacraments and other sacred actions, persons, or things in profane or unworthy ways. We refer to this as "sacrilege."

[18] Sixth, we should not attempt to buy or sell "spiritual things" such as prayers, healings, or sacred offices. Church ministers in particular should not charge a fee to pray for the dead or help the living. This is especially true of the sacraments, where no fee should be charged beyond that approved by the bishop, especially to the poor.

[19] Seventh, atheism is a serious matter in our time, and this commandment addresses it. There are several kinds of atheism. One kind is materialism, which places things above corporal works of mercy. Another kind is humanism, which considers us humans to be an end in ourselves with supreme control of our own history. A third kind looks to economics and social change to free humans, arguing that religion places too much hope in a future life and not enough in this one.

[20] We Christians can slow the rise of atheism by living authentically, practicing our own faith well, and teaching clearly our own beliefs. Finally, there is agnosticism. Agnostics claim "not to know and, therefore, not to care" about God; but really, it is intentional unbelief.

Images of God
[21] No one has ever seen God yet we believe God is the author of beauty, loveliness, and all creation. We humans are physical beings, needing signs and symbols to express our faith. Jesus himself was among us in physical form through the mystery of the Incarnation. So venerating an image of Christ or of Mary or the saints, or even of Creation itself, gives honor to the subject of the image, not to the image itself.

Group or personal process

- How is idolatry part of our social life today? What kind of idols do we have that lead us away from the one, true God?

- We have just learned that when we place possessions or power above the corporal or spiritual works of mercy, we are practicing a form of atheism. What is your experience of this?

- How do we Christians give witness to our faith in today's world? See faith statement #20 to understand this more clearly.

- Personally for you, what false gods do you need to confront in your life?

PART THREE ✛ ARTICLES 2142–2159 OF THE *CATECHISM*

The second commandment

[22] You shall not take the name of the Lord your God in vain. The second commandment calls us to respect the very name of God. The gift of one's name is personal and loving, a sign of deepening friendship and trust. God confided the divine name Yahweh to us, and we must revere it and keep it holy. Whenever we speak of God, it should be with reverence and respect and never with fear and threats.

[23] Nor should we use God's name or that of Mary and the saints to curse or make false promises. Nor should we speak against God with defiance or reproach in our speech, nor against the Church or sacred things. Nor should we act with violence toward others, using God's name as our cover or religion as our mantle.

[24] If we swear an oath taking God as our witness, it must be true and honest. A false oath calls on God to be witness to a lie. We refer to such false oaths as "perjury." Pledging oneself by oath to commit an evil deed is also contrary to the holiness of the divine name. Jesus teaches us to simply say what is true without recourse to an oath, but we have traditionally understood that for grave and right reasons an oath is acceptable, such as in court. But no oath should ever be sworn for a trivial matter.

WE BELIEVE

This commandment forbids the improper use of God's name, which is blasphemy. We are also forbidden from using the name of Jesus, Mary, or the saints in such a way.

Our name

[25] We Catholics bless ourselves, baptize each other, and live in the name of God. "In the name of the Father, and of the Son, and of the Holy Spirit. Amen." God's name sanctifies us and orients us.

[26] At birth and later in baptism, we too receive a name which is our sacred identity. Catholics are named according to Christian sentiment, often with a patron saint or after a Christian mystery or virtue. God calls each one of us by name, and each of our names is sacred. The name is the "icon of the person," and we should respect each other's names, honor them, protect them, and use them often!

Group or personal process

- In your own words, what does it mean to take God's name "in vain"? What are some ways in which you speak of God or think about God?

- We believe that God calls each one of us by name. In what ways has God called you? To what specific works of charity or mercy are you called?

Prayer

I give you thanks, O Lord, with my whole heart; before the gods I sing your praise; I bow down toward your holy temple and give thanks to your name for your steadfast love and your faithfulness; for you have exalted your name and your word above everything. On the day I called, you answered me; you increased my strength of soul. Amen. (**PSALM 138:1–3**)

Session Two

BASED ON ARTICLES 2168–2188 OF THE *CATECHISM OF THE CATHOLIC CHURCH*. TO READ A SUMMARY OF THIS SECTION, SEE *CATECHISM* ARTICLES 2189–2195

Introduction

The ceremonial observance of the "Sabbath" has been replaced by Sunday, which recalls the new creation inaugurated by the resurrection of Christ. Sunday is to be considered the foremost holy day of obligation in the universal Church. On Sundays, we are to avoid unnecessary labor and work, allowing time for family and friends. Every Christian should avoid making unnecessary demands on others that would hinder them from observing the Lord's Day.

Scripture

READER: A reading from the Book of Deuteronomy.

Observe the sabbath day and keep it holy, as the LORD your God commanded you. Six days you shall labor and do all your work. But the seventh day is a sabbath to the LORD your God; you shall not do any work—you, or your son or your daughter, or your male or female slave, or your ox or your donkey, or any of your livestock, or the resident alien in your towns, so that your male and female slave may rest as well as you. (**DEUTERONOMY 5:12–14**)

READER: The word of the Lord.

ALL: Thanks be to God.

PART ONE + **ARTICLES 2168–2176 OF THE** *CATECHISM*

Keeping holy

[1] "Remember the sabbath day and keep it holy," we read in Exodus, chapter 20, verse 8. "Six days you shall labor, and do all your work. But the seventh day is a sabbath to the LORD your God; you shall not do any work." This is the third commandment, and it is one that is often forgotten in our culture today.

[2] Using figurative language, the writers of the Old Testament picture God "resting" on the seventh day. The term "Sabbath" comes to us from the Hebrew *sabbat,* which means, literally, "to rest." Did God need to rest? In fact, from our earliest times, humans have had a need, deeply imbedded in human nature, to pause now and then to remember, to think back over recent events, to bring to mind God's hand in life, and to pray.

[3] The Sabbath is such a day, "a sacred pause in life," and it is so important to us humans that we consider it an obligation. For if we fail to pause and see what God has done, see how the world has unfolded before us, read the signs of the times, and take it all in, we may miss the most important part. The earth itself rests in this way as one season turns to another; one is for growing, and another for harvesting; one is for regenerating the fields, another for planting once again in springtime.

Jesus and the Sabbath

[4] The Gospel of Mark provides a peek into Jesus' own attitude toward the Sabbath. This gospel does not lollygag with angels and shepherds, or even with magi. It rushes headlong into Jesus' ministry. Within the first twenty verses of the first chapter Jesus has appeared on the scene, been baptized by John, gone out into and returned from his desert retreat, and called his first disciples; now, in verse 21, he appears in the synagogue in Capernaum, near his home town, on the Sabbath.

[5] Jesus taught that day with a sort of urgency, and he astounded the people. He showed tremendous power and authority healing the sick and caring for all. His teaching about the Sabbath and its place in life was revolutionary for his time: he insisted that keeping the letter of the law was not enough. The Sabbath is for humans, he insisted, not humans for the Sabbath. This is a day for doing good, rather than harm, for saving life rather than killing, a day of mercies, a day to honor God.

WE BELIEVE

The Church celebrates the day of the resurrection of the Lord on "the eighth day," which is rightly called the Lord's Day.

The Lord's Day

[6] Perhaps the psalmist best captures the spirit of this day: "This is the day that the LORD has made," we sing in Psalm 118, verse 24; "let us rejoice and be glad in it!"

[7] We Christians honor Sunday because on that day we commemorate Jesus' own resurrection from the dead. From the earliest years of Christian history, Sunday has been our day of days. The command-

ment to keep holy the Sabbath for us Christians means to observe Sunday as a day of rest, prayer, recreation, and shared meals.

Group or personal process

- What are the features of our modern culture that work against having a true day of rest on Sunday? How can we Christians best balance our faith with our culture regarding this?

- Talk together about your "Sunday habits" as a household or an individual. How can you adjust these habits to make "keeping holy the Sabbath" a higher priority?

PART TWO + ARTICLES 2177–2183 OF THE *CATECHISM*

The Sunday assembly

[8] For us Catholics, celebrating the Eucharist on Sunday is at the heart of how we observe the day. Canon law makes this clear in canon 1246, where it says that Sunday is the day on which the paschal mystery is celebrated. Sunday, canon law says, is "the foremost holy day of obligation in the universal Church."

[9] We also observe certain other "holy days," including Christmas and Epiphany, the Ascension, the feast of the Body and Blood of Christ, the feast of Mary, the Mother of God, her Assumption, her Immaculate Conception, the feasts of Saints Joseph, Peter and Paul, and the feast of All Saints.

[10] On certain feasts Catholics have an obligation to attend the

Eucharist. We assemble for the Eucharist on these days, week in and week out, because the Eucharist is our lifeblood. Participating each week, gathering with each other, hearing the word broken open and shared, offering and blessing our gifts, remembering the story of the Lord's Supper, receiving communion, and being sent in peace—this is who we are, this is the body of Christ.

WE BELIEVE

On Sundays and certain holy days, the faithful are bound to rest from their labor as much as possible. Sunday is the foremost holy day in the Church, and we are obliged to participate in the Mass on this day.

---

[11] It becomes a cadence in our everyday lives, a drum beat, and a regular rhythm in life. We gather as a parish, a particular and definite community, guided by a pastor who is supported by a bishop. This is the gathering place where all the faithful come from their own homes to share in the liturgical actions. Praying at home is important but we also need to pray together. The pastors of the Church require us to do this, to participate in Mass each week, anywhere in any Catholic rite on the day itself or on the evening before.

[12] There may from time to time be a serious reason why it is not possible for us to participate in Mass, such as illness or the care of the sick. But for those who make a pattern of being absent, of excusing themselves for minor reasons, or of simply not attending because they don't agree with the Church or don't like the pastor or don't want to give up a morning, or don't feel they receive any benefits from it, or for any other reason, this is a serious matter.

[13] Eucharist is our foundation, the heart of our faith, and our very identity. To skip it on a regular basis sets up a pattern that will

not produce in us a deep well of spiritual well-being. It is not only for ourselves that we participate in the Sunday assembly. It is also for our neighbors and friends who depend on us to be present and share faith with them.

[14] Even if we feel our own faith is rather thin or that our hearts will not be in it, simply by being in the room, by being in that place where grace is shared, we will be touched. A single word in the homily will awaken an insight—or a whiff of candle wax or incense, or the sight of all in the communion procession, or a refrain of music.

[15] Christ is present in the Eucharist in a fourfold way: in the word that is shared, in the community gathered, in the person of the priest, and in the bread and wine, hosts to the Body and Blood of Christ. If no priest is present for any reason, the faithful can gather with the word, following the guidelines of the local bishop.

Group or personal process

- Why is it important to gather each week to celebrate the Eucharist? What prevents people from doing this?

- Make a list of those folks who either do not feel welcome or do not feel motivated to be a regular part of the Sunday assembly in your parish. How could you as a parish reach out to these people to welcome them or make them feel comfortable, or to help create a desire for the Eucharist in their lives?

- How does being part of the community for Mass each week contribute to your spiritual life? What do you give to your community, and what do you take away from being there?

Rest

[16] Participating in Mass on Sundays and holy days of obligation does not totally fulfill the requirement of this commandment to "keep holy" the Sabbath. In order for us humans to be whole and healthy, we need a pattern of rest from work. We need time to celebrate family times, household meals, cultural events, social engagements, and quiet times of rest, reading, and prayer.

[17] Perhaps the most important activity we humans crave is to share meals together. Whether we're rich or poor, urban or rural, young or old, there is a deep human need to "recline at table with friends." The shared meal is as ancient as the human family and as sacred as the liturgy.

WE BELIEVE

Every Christian should avoid making unnecessary demands on others that would hinder them from observing the Lord's Day.

[18] Therefore, the pastors of the Church require us to refrain from any work or activity on Sundays that would limit the time we have to spend together at table. While there may be legitimate reasons to work on Sunday such as family needs, important social services, or tending to the sick or otherwise needy, we should be careful not to let these exceptions create a rule whereby we work on Sunday just as on any other day.

[19] This is perhaps the most difficult commandment for modern Christians to observe because Sunday in our culture is compromised by materialism, consumerism, and secularism.

[20] There is also the situation where some of us must work simply because we are so poor. Our jobs require us to work on Sunday, and to keep the job we must comply. For many people in today's culture around the world, balancing the demand of earning a sufficient income for the needs of family and children with the more personal needs of one's own life is very difficult if not impossible. This is often especially true of single parents, the materially poor, immigrants, and those entering the workforce for the first time.

[21] When we spend leisure time on Sunday in public places such as parks, sporting events, shopping centers, restaurants, and the like, others must work to allow us to do that. Even though this is true, those who must work on those days should set aside time on another day for rest and leisure. All of us should recreate on Sundays with moderation, and we should be sensitive to what others must do to support our leisure activities. Employers should make sure that workers have sufficient time for rest.

[22] There is a tendency in modern times to operate business concerns on a twenty-four-hours-per-day, seven-days-per-week basis. Many businesses no longer observe Sunday at all. We Christians should address this by demonstrating the validity of our beliefs rather than condemning others. If we live as we should and allow others to see us, the world will come to a sacred pause and all will rest on Sundays as they are able and with tremendous joy.

Group or personal process

- In your household life, how do you observe Sunday beyond participating at Eucharist? How do you help or hinder others from doing so?

- Read faith statement #19 again. How can we learn to balance our busy lives and busy weeks with the commandment to rest on Sunday and to also allow others to rest?

Prayer

I thank you that you have answered me and have become my salvation. The stone that the builders rejected has become the chief cornerstone. This is the LORD's doing; it is marvelous in our eyes. This is the day that the LORD has made; let us rejoice and be glad in it. Save us, we beseech you, O LORD! O LORD, we beseech you, give us success! Blessed is the one who comes in the name of the LORD. We bless you from the house of the LORD. The LORD is God, and he has given us light. Amen. (**PSALM 118:21–27**)

Session Three

HONORING OUR PARENTS: *the 4ᵗʰ commandment*

BASED ON ARTICLES 2196–2246 OF THE *CATECHISM OF THE CATHOLIC CHURCH*. TO READ A SUMMARY OF THIS SECTION, SEE *CATECHISM* ARTICLES 2247–2257

Introduction

According to the fourth commandment, God has willed that we should honor our parents and those whom he has vested with authority for our good. Children owe their parents respect, gratitude, just obedience, and assistance. Parents have the first responsibility for the education of their children in the faith, prayer, and all the virtues. They have the duty to provide as far as possible for the physical and spiritual needs of their children. It is the duty of citizens to work with civil authority for building up society in a spirit of truth, justice, solidarity, and freedom.

Scripture

READER: A reading from the Book of Deuteronomy.

Honor your father and your mother, as the LORD your God commanded you, so that your days may be long and that it may go well with you in the land that the LORD your God is giving you. (**DEUTERONOMY 5:16**)

READER: The word of the Lord.

ALL: Thanks be to God.

Parents and children

[1] You might have noticed by now that the Christian life is based on one thing: God's abundant mercy and love. The fourth commandment is rooted in that love. "Honor your father and your mother," it says in Exodus, chapter 20, verse 12, "so that your days may be long in the land which the LORD your God is giving you."

[2] This is a commandment for children, that is, anyone with parents. We do not choose our parents, of course, but we believe that we should respect them and all others who are in authority. This commandment forms the foundation for life in an orderly society. It is part of the social doctrine of the Church today.

WE BELIEVE
The purposes and aims of marriage and family life are to support the goodness and love of the spouses and to bear and educate children.

---

[3] Traditionally this commandment has been held to extend beyond children and parents to all elders and ancestors in one's family, to give them affection and honor, care and gratitude, throughout their lives.

[4] It extends in tradition to students and their teachers, to citizens and their governments, to employees and their superiors, to members of the Church and its pastors. This is the first commandment which brings a reward: if you do this, you will have long life. Indeed, failing to observe this command results in unhappiness and social breakdown.

The family

[5] In Catholic teaching, marriage has two purposes: to support the mutual love of the couple and to bring children into the world. A man and woman committed in marriage together with their children form a family. Other forms of family relationships also exist, but this is the norm. Families have many responsibilities and rights and form the basic building block of society.

[6] This family, together with other relatives, neighbors, friends, and visitors, forms a sort of "household of faith" and is rightly called by a name, "domestic church." We use a particular terminology to refer to families when we call them a "communion of persons"—a sign and image of the shared life of the Trinity: God who is Father, Christ the Son, and the Holy Spirit.

[7] Having children is a reflection of God's work of creation. Healthy and generous "dying to ourselves" in family life connects us with Christ in his own dying and rising known as the paschal mystery. And being joined in deep unity and solidarity is a gift of the Spirit to households of faith. This is a privileged sharing in the life of the Triune God.

Society and family

[8] Family life is rehearsal for life in society for the children and a way of life rooted in love and self-giving for the parents. In the family we share moral values, we learn to honor and love God, and we learn the limits of freedom. Families should care for the young and the old, the sick, handicapped, and poor. Where the family cannot do this alone, other social bodies should provide assistance.

[9] Governments should do whatever is needed to strengthen and protect family life. Among other things, governments should provide

the freedom to establish a family and have children, the freedom to follow religious convictions, the protection of the marriage bond, the right to private property, free enterprise, work and housing, emigration rights, medical care, assistance for the aged, the protection of financial security, and the freedom to form associations.

[10] But legislation alone isn't enough. Society must be oriented toward social values that support households of faith. And households of faith should likewise support the society in which they live. In this way all relationships can be built up and made strong, and we will live as children of God.

Group or personal process

- Who lives in your "household of faith"? How is that household a reflection of the love of God?

- What challenges are there to establishing warm and loving family life these days?

- Name two or three activities that families can do on a regular basis that support family life.

PART TWO + ARTICLES 2214–2231 OF THE *CATECHISM*
The duties of children

[11] The respect and honor which a child is called upon to bestow on his or her parents flows from the fatherhood and motherhood of God and is an obligation that lasts a lifetime. The books of wisdom in the Bible remind us time and again of this duty, and the

early Christian teachings do the same. "My child, keep your father's commandment," we read, for example, in Proverbs, chapter 6, "and do not forsake your mother's teaching. Bind them upon your heart always; tie them around your neck. When you walk, they will lead you; when you lie down, they will watch over you; and when you awake, they will talk with you."

[12] Children should likewise obey their parents unless the child is convinced in conscience that it would be morally wrong to do so, as article 2217 of the *Catechism* reminds us. And when children are grown and living on their own, they should still respect their parents: care for them in old age and love them in times of distress and loneliness, even though the obligation to obey them ceases when the child becomes an adult.

[13] Family life should be filled with harmony and love, not only between parents and children but among the children and grandchildren, and even among visitors and neighbors.

WE BELIEVE

*Parents should respect and encourage
their children's calling, helping them become
the persons God wants them to be.
The first calling is to follow Jesus.*

The duties of parents

[14] Simply bearing children is not all there is to being a parent. There is much more at stake in raising a family: teaching love by loving, teaching faith by believing, and teaching care for the poor by practicing it—teaching, teaching, teaching. Indeed, the role of parents in the education of their children is so important that it's

almost impossible to find an adequate substitute!

[15] Parents provide this education for children by first creating a household of faith where tenderness, forgiveness, respect, fidelity, and generous self-giving are the norm. The household is where children are apprenticed, as it were, in self-denial and dying to selfishness, in making good judgments, and in growing in age and wisdom.

[16] Parents and other teachers within the household help children understand the importance of spirituality and the inner life in addition to material goods. Children learn by good example, by being apprentices, so it is important for parents to admit when they're wrong, to be fully honest about their own failings, and to be quick to forgive and carry no grudge.

[17] Parents are also called upon, of course, to pass on to their children their own faith. They should join with a parish community and initiate their children through baptism. By making their faith part of family life, children will grow to know Jesus and love the Church.

[18] Household-based catechesis is shaped and helped by parish-level catechesis and formation, but what happens in the household is vital. Children learn to pray from their parents; they learn to love the materially poor, to love the Eucharist, and to embrace the gospel fully.

[19] And children, in turn, contribute to the growth of their parents' faith. Within a household, all should be quick to forgive; all should handle disagreements with grace, avoid injustices within the family, and offer each other mutual affection. Indeed, the charity of Christ demands nothing less.

[20] Parents should choose schools for their children which assure they will be well educated. And when they become adults, children have a right to choose their profession with the advice and assistance

of their parents, and parents should support the vocation that their children follow. Some children will choose to follow a religious vocation, or to enter the priesthood, and some to remain single for life, or others to take on other vocational choices. Remember always that the first vocation for everyone is to follow Christ.

Group or personal process

- Shared prayer can be difficult in family life. Family members may pray differently or at different times from one another. How and when can a family or household realistically share reflective and prayerful moments?

- In your parish community, what do the households look like? Make a chart showing the makeup of your parish and include on it the numbers of people living in single-parent households, two-parent households, ecumenical households (where one spouse is not Catholic), widow and widower households, single-adult households, and so forth. How does your parish support "family life" in all its many forms?

PART THREE + ARTICLES 2232–2246 OF THE *CATECHISM*
Civil society and the fourth commandment

[21] Church teaching on the fourth commandment also extends to the duties of civil authorities and the duties of citizens within a nation, and we will consider that next.

[22] All authority, whether within the Church or in government, should be exercised as a service. We believe that all such authority comes, in the first place, from God alone. Therefore, no one can command or establish anything that is contrary to the dignity of persons or the natural law.

[23] Furthermore, those in authority must organize society with values according to the norms of justice for all and in such a way that the common good is pursued, and not merely for personal gain for themselves or for anyone. Political rights should be respected and should not be suspended unless there is a prevailing reason to do so, and then only on a temporary basis.

[24] For their part, citizens should trust authority and collaborate with it for the common good. When it is right to do so, citizens should criticize government, especially when harm is being done to anyone anywhere at any time or when human dignity is not respected. Citizens should take roles in the public domain, helping govern their nations with justice.

WE BELIEVE

Public authority must respect the fundamental rights of each human person. People must be free to have families, practice their faith, and possess a home and the means for a livelihood.

---

[25] Citizens should pay their taxes, vote when the time comes, and defend their country if necessary. Wealthy nations are obliged under justice to welcome foreigners and immigrants, to share their wealth generously and fairly, and to protect those in harm's way.

[26] Christian citizens are obliged in conscience not to follow their government when what is demanded is contrary to moral order, to fundamental human rights, or to the teachings of the gospel. Civil disobedience of this sort is justified in the distinction between serving God and serving the political community. Still, even in these cases, citizens should support whatever works toward the common good, even while defending human rights against the abuse of unjust authority.

[27] Before taking up arms against political authority, the following conditions must all be met: There must be certain, grave, and prolonged violation of fundamental human rights. All other means of setting things right have been exhausted, and such resistance will not make things worse. There is a well-founded hope of success, few victims will suffer who are innocent, and it is impossible to foresee a better way out.

[28] We believe that the welfare of human persons is always the priority in any society. Our human source and destiny, after all, is in God. Rulers that fail to recognize this and who place property, power, money, or material goods in a place of higher priority than human beings are totalitarian and evil.

[29] Finally, we want to point out that the Church is not the same as the political community. The Church, in a way, transcends the culture and society in which she lives, calling everyone to the same standard: the protection and advancement of the human race. Toward this end, the pastors of the Church make judgments and teach clearly regarding the morality of politics and government, especially when the fundamental rights of people are at stake.

Group or personal process

- What aspects of the government in the nation where you live are at odds with protecting the fundamental rights of every human person? What stance do you as a Christian take regarding that?

- How much pressure can Christians bring to their government to follow Christian principles when we live in a society made up of people from many faith traditions?

Prayer

In your wisdom, Lord, you teach us to honor and obey our parents and those who become our teachers and mentors. Thank you for those whom you have brought into my life for this purpose. Guard and protect them as they grow older. For those who have died, I pray that they may rest in peace in your bosom. May I now become such a parent, mentor, or teacher for others, and may your grace lead me to reflect you in all I do. Through Christ, our Lord. Amen.

Session Four

BASED ON ARTICLES 2258–2317 OF THE *CATECHISM OF THE CATHOLIC CHURCH*. TO READ A SUMMARY OF THIS SECTION, SEE *CATECHISM* ARTICLES 2318–2330

Introduction

Every human life, from the moment of conception until death, is sacred because the human person is created in the image and likeness of God. The murder of a human being is gravely contrary to the dignity of the person and the holiness of the Creator. We are bound to reject abortion, to protect the embryo, and to defend life in every other way. The death penalty is normally against church teaching as well. The arms race is one of the greatest curses on the human race, and the harm it inflicts on the poor is more than can be endured.

Scripture

READER: A reading from the Gospel of Matthew.

"You have heard that it was said to those of ancient times, 'You shall not murder'; and 'whoever murders shall be liable to judgment.' But I say to you that if you are angry with a brother or sister, you will be liable to judgment; and if you insult a brother or sister, you will be liable to the council." (**MATTHEW 5:21–22A**)

READER: The word of the Lord.

ALL: Thanks be to God.

You shall not kill

[1] The four words that make up this commandment are simple, straightforward, and clear. Their deep meaning is at the foundation of how we treat each other. And yet, it might not be quite as clear as it sounds. Jesus added a new layer of complexity to this when he taught in the Sermon on the Mount, "You have heard that it was said...'You shall not murder'...But I say to you that if you are angry with a brother or sister, you will be liable to judgment." What does this mean? Is anger equal to murder?

[2] We Catholics defend human life in all stages because we are made in God's image and we have been given God's own life. We believe that life unfolds for us all from beginning to end with the spiritual energy and power of God. This commandment makes it clear that no one may deliberately interrupt that flow of life, nor even cause pain and suffering for others.

[3] We humans have an inclination to selfishness, to fear, anger, and aggression, to being completely unilateral at times, completely one-sided. This dark inclination seems to have been present from the beginning, as the figurative story of Abel and Cain suggests.

[4] In reading the human heart Jesus takes this entire matter even further, realizing, perhaps, that we don't begin by being murderers. We begin with envy and anger. Therefore, Jesus teaches us to turn the other cheek, to love our enemies, and to forgive seventy times seven times. He chose not to defend himself even though he was innocent, and he told Peter not to use the sword. In short, Jesus shifted the ground of this question to love.

Legitimate defense

[5] There is a delicate balance that must be sought between defending against aggression and injustice and defending life at all times, even that of one's enemy. We are bound, the pastors of the Church teach, to defend ourselves and those under our care and to prevent those perpetrating injustice from overtaking society and the world. This is true for the sake of the common good both personally and nationally.

[6] Even if this means killing others in violent self-defense it is permitted for the Christian; but any violence and killing must be minimal, deemed absolutely necessary, and not include the innocent bystander. We must discern carefully in our day and age to be sure that those defending themselves, who are often the very rich, are not the ones perpetrating injustice themselves in the first place.

WE BELIEVE

The murder of any human being is gravely contrary to the dignity with which we are created and the holiness to which we are called.

Capital punishment

[7] We believe that the state has the right to punish people who commit crimes with a punishment that matches the gravity of the original crime. As far as possible such punishment should contribute to the correction of the offender. Whenever possible this punishment should be bloodless because that better corresponds to human dignity.

[8] Given the means at the state's disposal in these times to imprison offenders and render them inoffensive, we teach that cases in which the death penalty is suitable and permitted are rare if practically

non-existent. On this point, the original edition of the *Catechism* has been amended to better clarify our teaching.

Intentional homicide

[9] Intentional killing is not permitted, and doing so is gravely sinful. The killing of one's children or siblings, parents or spouse, is especially heinous. One may not even expose another to mortal danger, hence causing death indirectly, and we must always assist those in such danger. For example, when famine occurs, we must remedy it and may not sit on the sidelines, hoping for better weather and crops. To fail to assist the materially poor is to commit indirect homicide, according to article 2269 of the *Catechism*.

Group or personal process

- Define injustice. How does it cause violence and war? How do we eliminate or reduce it in our human family?

- How can we embrace the Church's teaching on the death penalty more fully?

- Read an edition of today's newspaper from a major city. Circle the instances that concern injustice, murder, and the taking of innocent life. How could your parish as a whole, or the individual members of your parish, help to end the bloodshed?

Issues of life and death

Abortion

[10] When the prophet Jeremiah received his call, it came to him as a word of the Lord, spoken perhaps in the recesses of his heart. These words still inspire awe in us: "Before I formed you in the womb, I knew you." We believe that, at the moment of conception, God speaks a single, unique word through the love of the spouses and the generosity of the mother. That word spoken by God is nothing less than *the life of the one conceived.* We humans are partners in this creative divine love, and we should never be reckless about conception.

[11] The Church has always taught that intentionally having an abortion is morally wrong. From the earliest years of the Christian community it has been prohibited, along with killing newborn children. Likewise, cooperating in having an abortion is wrong. And, while the pastors of the Church condemn this, the Church does not intend to limit the scope of God's mercy.

[12] The pastors of the Church want to make very clear the irreparable harm done to the unborn child, the grave harm done in the spiritual life of the parents, the degrading of society, the general social climate that treats life so dismissively and trivially that it threatens, in turn, the common good. Because this is so serious, the Church teaches that those who take part in having abortions, provided it was their free choice and they understood the gravity of this choice, effectively remove themselves from the Church, that is, from the body of Christ.

[13] Until they recognize their error and offense and make amends, they are outside the Church itself. We should remember that there

may be psychological factors, or sociological ones, that prevent some people from having full freedom when making the choice to abort a pregnancy.

[14] We believe that the state should protect all those who have been conceived and certainly should not encourage abortion as a means of limiting population. And, in order to maintain deep reverence for all life, we oppose producing embryos with the intention of abusing or destroying them. We also support social programs that provide care for the parents who are pregnant to assist them medically and socially.

WE BELIEVE

Every human being has the right to a dignified and full life from conception to natural death.

Euthanasia

[15] People who are sick deserve special love and care. We believe that intentionally killing someone, even if it is to end pain and suffering, is morally wrong. One may, however, refuse medical treatments, or bring them to an end, if they are burdensome or dangerous, extraordinary or disproportionate to the outcome. In these cases, one does not cause death but simply accepts its inevitability.

[16] The patient should decide this if he or she is capable, and if not, then the decison is made by those in whose care the patient resides; the patient's reasonable will and legitimate interests must always be respected. Using painkilling and calming drugs is permitted, even at the risk of shortening life, provided the motive is not to end life but to bring comfort.

Suicide

[17] We are stewards of our lives, not owners. Our lives are a gift to us from the heart of God and we should honor them and care for them. Our lives are not ours to dispose of willy-nilly. Therefore, we teach that suicide is wrong. It is unilateral, that is, one-sided, and it causes tremendous suffering in one's family and friends. Like other forms of killing, it breaks down the holy order of the common good. So committing suicide, or helping someone else do it, is outside any Christian lifestyle.

[18] At the same time, the pastors of the Church recognize that sometimes people face seemingly insurmountable life situations, suffer from mental illness, give up hope for one reason or another, or fear hardship or torture. We trust in God's mercy above all and we hope and pray for those who do this, but we do not condemn them.

Scandal

[19] The term "scandal" comes from Greek, where it means, literally, "stumbling block." When we place a stumbling block in front of someone, tempting them, for example, to join in evil, or to avoid love and doing what is good, we "scandalize them." This is always morally wrong and Jesus had a stern warning for anyone who does this.

[20] Scandal can be a largely personal offense, or it can be institutional and public. Employers, for example, who encourage dishonesty or groups that tolerate gossip are causing scandal. Teachers who provoke their students to anger or parents who fail to create households of faith are causing scandal. Wealthy citizens who hoard their money and property or business leaders who permit fraud are causing scandal.

[21] *Anyone* who uses the power at his or her disposal in such a way that it leads others to do wrong becomes guilty of scandal. "Occasions for stumbling are bound to come," Jesus taught in Luke, chapter 17, verse 1, "but woe to anyone by whom they come!"

Respect for health

[22] The care of people's health is a vital element in building up the common good, and society has a duty to provide for it along with other basic needs: food and clothing, housing and education, employment and social assistance. We are obliged, however, as individuals, to avoid abusing food, alcohol, tobacco, or drugs. If we are addicted, we should seek help. If we are selling and profiting from illegal drugs, we are giving scandal and cooperating in evil.

Scientific medical research

[23] We recognize that research contributes to healing, and we support the advancement of public health. Such research promotes human dignity and should be celebrated. The principles that guide such research arise from belief about human beings—that we have certain rights and needs. All research must serve humans and not hurt them either by experimentation that is harmful or by taking risks that are dangerous. Organ transplants are wonderful and holy acts provided the donor has died naturally or accidentally and the recipient has a reasonable chance of survival.

Torture and terrorism

[24] Kidnapping and hostage taking are terrible threats and, of course, are not permitted to Christians. Likewise, terrorism—either personal or social—is gravely against justice and charity. Torture is never permitted, either to extract information, to punish those judged guilty, to frighten opponents, or to satisfy hatred and re-

venge. Likewise, dismembering a living human being, except for medical reasons, is always completely wrong.

[25] In the past, such cruel practices were common and were used by governments, without protest from the pastors of the Church. Indeed, the pastors of the Church themselves used such measures in their own courts and practices, especially during the years of the Inquisition. In recent times it has become evident that these cruel practices were neither necessary for public order nor in conformity with the legitimate rights of the human person. On the contrary, these practices led to ones even more degrading. We regret this now and see our error and are working to end this everywhere.

Respect for the dead

[26] Those who are dying should be given care, comfort, and prayerful attention. At the appropriate time they should be offered the sacraments that prepare them for death. The burial of the dead is a corporal work of mercy. Autopsies are permitted either for legal inquiries or for medical research. Donating one's organs is a generous final gift of life. Cremation is permitted for Catholics.

Group or personal process

- Why do you think it is so difficult for us humans to have a consistent ethic of life, ranging from feeding the hungry and caring for women with children, to protecting the end and the beginning of life?

- Care for our own bodies is an expression of living this commandment. What does this mean, in practical terms? How do we violate this commandment in terms of physical and mental health?

- Scandal is a serious sin against this commandment. Describe some situations that could occur in the course of daily life where we might take part in this kind of activity.

PART THREE + ARTICLES 2302–2317 OF THE *CATECHISM*

Blessed are the peacemakers

[27] This commandment teaches us a central lesson regarding how we manage our passions and how we control and heal our emotions. For if we are angry with someone and we allow that anger to fester and grow so that it reaches a point where we desire to kill them, where we want vengeance or we want to punish them or seriously wound them, we have crossed the line, and we are in grave sinfulness. In that case, we have allowed our emotions to make us completely unilateral. We often become like the enemy we wish to trounce.

[28] On the other hand, if we allow our anger to create in us a desire to bring justice to bear, to teach the greater truth of love and peace, then we are living in charity. Deliberate hatred is contrary to charity. Cultivating hatred of one's neighbor or enemy is a grave wrong because it is so unloving. Even if the enemy attacks you, hatred can never be condoned. In fact, the way to peace is charity and love and the careful cultivation within our hearts of feelings which lead to that.

[29] We Catholics believe that peace is more than the absence of war. It is not limited to maintaining a "balance of powers" between adversaries, whether on the personal, local, or national levels. No, peace is clearly the work of justice. We must safeguard the goods of persons, their free communication and free thought, respect for

their human dignity, and tireless practice of seeking the common good. Peace is the work of justice and the outcome of charity. Such peace is possible through grace, through the powerful love of Christ.

Avoiding war

[30] The pastors of the Church urge all people to seek peace through works of justice that safeguard all people and through actions to avoid war. The obligation to seek other solutions belongs to everyone, but if all else fails, governments may engage in lawful self-defense. Strict conditions for such self-defense must be met, and because of the gravity of war, this must be a rigorously made decision.

[31] The *Catechism* outlines these conditions in article 2309. All of these conditions must be met in order to justify war: "the damage inflicted by the aggressor on the nation or community of nations must be lasting, grave, and certain; all other means of putting an end to it must have been shown to be impractical or ineffective; there must be serious prospects of success; the use of arms must not produce evils and disorders graver than the evil to be eliminated."

WE BELIEVE

Because of the evil and injustice that war brings with it, we must do all we can to avoid or end war. The arms race is a great curse on the human family.

---

[32] Because of the power and devastation of modern war, and because of the size of modern bombs, meeting these conditions is very difficult if not impossible today. We call these conditions the traditional "just war" doctrine.

[33] Governments have the right and duty to ask their citizens to work in national defense, and those sworn to do so are servants of the common good. But governments must also make provision so that those who, for reasons of conscience, refuse to bear arms or enter into violence can serve in another way.

[34] During war, moral law still prevails. War does not mean that suddenly everything becomes lawful and morally good. The innocent citizen bystanders, for example, along with the wounded and the prisoner, must be respected and treated properly. Any order for an action which is contrary to moral law or international law does not have to be followed.

[35] Simply obeying a command does not excuse an individual from committing a grave crime. So, for example, genocide is morally wrong, or rape of the enemy, or indiscriminate destruction of entire cities. The end does not justify the means.

[36] A real danger of modern warfare is that it provides the opportunity to those who possess modern weapons, especially atomic, biological, or chemical weapons, to commit such crimes. We Catholics have strong moral reservations that the doctrine of deterrence can effectively win the peace. Actually, it brings the risk of war to greater intensity because it does not eliminate the causes of hatred, aggression, and animosity. It uses up scarce resources that should go to the poor, and it elevates our sense of insecurity. Some leaders even traffic in fear, using it to encourage public trust in them.

[37] Again, the pathway to peace is justice, rooted in charity. What causes war are injustice, excessive economic or social inequalities, envy, distrust, and pride among people and nations.

Group or personal process

- How can we as individuals participate in peacemaking? How do we contribute to war?

- We often feel as though there is nothing we as individuals or small groups can do to create peace and end war. Is this accurate? Why or why not?

- When have wars in the past been justified? When have they been wrongfully started and fought? What is your personal experience of such wars?

Prayer

O Lord, you have set before us today life and prosperity, death and adversity. Help us to obey the commandments you give us by loving you with all our hearts, walking in your ways, and observing your commandments, decrees, and ordinances. We know that we will live and become numerous, and you, Lord, will bless us in the land where we live. Keep our heart from turning away from you. We pray through Christ, our Lord. Amen. (**FROM DEUTERONOMY 30:15–17**)

Session Five

BASED ON ARTICLES 2331–2391 AND 2514–2527 OF THE CATECHISM OF THE CATHOLIC CHURCH. TO READ A SUMMARY OF THIS SECTION, SEE CATECHISM ARTICLES 2392–2400 AND 2528–2533

Introduction

By creating the human being man and woman, God gives personal dignity to the one and the other. Each of them, man and woman, should acknowledge and accept his or her sexual identity. Chastity means the full and complete integration of sexuality within the person. The covenant that spouses have freely entered into entails faithful love. It imposes on them the obligation to keep their marriage indissoluble. The ninth commandment warns against lust or carnal concupiscence.

Scripture

READER: A reading from the Gospel of Matthew.

"You have heard that it was said, 'You shall not commit adultery.' But I say to you that everyone who looks at a woman [or man] with lust has already committed adultery with her [or him] in his [or her] heart. If your right eye causes you to sin, tear it out and throw it away; it is better for you to lose one of your members than for your whole body to be thrown into hell. And if your right hand causes you to sin, cut it off and throw it away; it is better for you to lose one of your members than for your whole body to go into hell." (**MATTHEW 5:27–30**)

READER: The word of the Lord.

ALL: Thanks be to God.

God is love

[1] The sixth commandment, on the face of it, sounds like one of those "shalt nots" but, in fact, it's a positive call to love deeply, profoundly, and divinely. "You shall not commit adultery," we read in Exodus, chapter 20, verse 14. Jesus added to this in his famous "sermon on the mount" in Matthew, chapters 5—7, where he taught that, beyond this commandment, even harboring lust in one's heart is adultery.

[2] We believe that God wrote into our own hearts a certain *vocation,* a vocation which every man and woman receives, and it is a vocation to love. In a real sense, this is a calling to be like God because, as we just said, God is love. Our sexuality is intended for love and for having children, two aims that must be held in balance when a man and woman marry.

[3] Our sexuality affects every aspect of life for us humans. The *Catechism* reminds us in article 2333 that "everyone, man and woman, should acknowledge and accept his [or her] sexual identity." There are differences between men and women as well as sameness; the harmony of society depends on how well we live that out and balance it. Men and women have equal personal dignity. Each is an image of the power and the tenderness of God. By joining together in marriage, they echo the love of God.

Chastity

[4] To be chaste is to successfully integrate one's sexuality within oneself, creating an inner unity between body and spirituality. Sexuality is physical. It becomes truly human when it is integrated into a loving relationship of one person to another in lifelong commitment.

[5] Chastity leads us to maintain the purpose and goals of the powers of life and love that are within us. It opposes any duplicity of life or speech that threatens or violates that purpose and goal. We must learn chastity. Either we do so and find peace, or we are dominated by passions and are unhappy. We must work against the idea—common today—that "anything goes." Indeed, in order for us humans to be whole and healthy, we must be self-aware, self-sacrificing, prayerful, faithful, single-hearted, and committed.

WE BELIEVE

Chastity means the full integration of one's sexuality into what it means to be a person. It includes learning how to live with self-control.

[6] Learning to live within our boundaries is essential, but it requires a lifelong effort. In this effort we pass through stages of growth, building ourselves up as free persons, deeply engaged with God and the Church. We gradually become more and more loving. Education should reflect the moral and spiritual aspects of human life in all its dimensions. Remember, in the end, it is the Holy Spirit who gives us the grace of chastity.

[7] We give ourselves to each other in love, and the ability to freely give our truest self is developed through the practice of chastity. Chastity, in other words, flows from charity, and both lead us to

God. Chastity blossoms in friendship that allows us to give ourselves to each other. As the *Catechism* reminds us in article 2347, "Whether it develops between persons of the same or opposite sex, friendship represents a great good for all. It leads to spiritual communion."

Group or personal process

• How do we learn about chastity as we grow throughout our lives toward greater and greater love and friendship?

• How does one "integrate one's sexuality" into the fabric of his or her life?

• How does the culture and society in which you live either contribute to or challenge your call to chastity?

PART TWO + **ARTICLES 2348–2379 OF THE *CATECHISM***

All are called

[8] Baptism implies in it a call to be chaste, in keeping with our state of life. Some people consecrate themselves to celibacy, which enables them to love and serve in a particular and generous way. Others choose to remain single throughout life. And many people marry, and in that case, chastity becomes a part of sexual activity. The Church has always taught that all these states of life are to be considered equally praiseworthy.

Challenges to chastity

[9] When we speak of lust as a serious sin in human life, we do so because it is unilateral in nature; it is one-sided. If we seek sexual pleasure only for ourselves in selfish and self-absorbed ways aside from its procreative and loving aspects, we are in lust.

[10] Masturbation is usually unilateral in this way; it is a one-sided sexual activity without the *self-giving* that gives life meaning. When we judge ourselves on this, we should take into account our emotional maturity, the force of habits we have acquired, and conditions of anxiety and other psychological factors. These may reduce or even eliminate the moral vice involved.

[11] Sexual intercourse between unmarried partners, which is called by the name "fornication," seems to violate human dignity and often leads to one person using the other for selfish and unilateral reasons. Pornography is entirely unilateral, almost completely without love in it at all. There is no intimate giving of persons to each other; in pornography one person uses another for selfish and unilateral reasons.

[12] Prostitution is also unilateral, one party using the other, even for money, to get short-term pleasure. In prostitution, both parties are hurt deeply, but the provider may not always be to blame since he or she may be destitute or under fear of being hurt by the employer.

[13] Rape is not so much a sin of sexuality and chastity as it is of violence. One may never make a moral case for rape saying that, in this or that occasion, it is morally good. It is always gravely sinful. Even more terrible is the rape of children.

Chastity and homosexuality

[14] Some people experience an exclusive attraction toward persons of their same gender. This is called "homosexuality," and throughout

history there have been many forms of it. It seems resistant to change and is deeply rooted in people. The Church does not condone sexual activity between gay and lesbian people. However, there are many women and men who experience this deep-seated orientation.

[15] No one chooses to be gay or lesbian. As article 2358 of the *Catechism* reminds us, they are to be respected and treated with compassion and care, and all discrimination against them should end. Like everyone else, gay and lesbian people are called to live in chastity within their friendships.

Chastity and marriage

[16] Sexual love within marriage is not merely a biological act. It is laced with deep meaning and spirituality; it concerns the innermost being of the person. We believe and teach that it loses its meaning and wounds the human spirit unless it occurs only between a man and woman who have committed themselves for life. Sexual loving is noble and honorable; it entails self-giving and generosity; it enriches the spouses with joy and pleasure.

[17] Sexual loving has two aims: the mutual love of the spouses and the conception of children. In marriage, the man and woman give themselves to each other for life and promise to remain faithful until death. They become, as Scripture says, "one flesh."

[18] Marriage fidelity echoes God's fidelity to us. Here two people take each other into their arms and say, in essence, "You are everything to me." Here two people share the same dream, plan to *spend* their lives, not waste them, by spending them generously on the needs of each other, their children, and their neighbors. Here two people place each other's need above their own, becoming of one mind and heart.

[19] The gift of a child to a married couple rises from deep within them, from their own mutual love and the sexual loving they share. It is an implied part of each and every sexual act; hence, every sexual act must be open to it. Married couples have and raise children, educating them, loving them, caring for them, and extending their own mutual love to their children.

[20] Because this is a large and all-encompassing activity, couples may wish to regulate and space births. If this is not a selfish desire on their part, it is right and noble to do so and is part of responsible parenthood. The methods with which they do this must be holy ones.

WE BELIEVE

The covenant into which spouses enter at marriage entails permanent, monogamous, freely given, and faithful love.

---

[21] The Church teaches that couples should, as much as possible and in keeping with their own consciences, enjoy sexual loving and regulate conception within the rhythm of fertile cycles, a practice known in various ways as natural family planning. The state should never usurp the rights of couples to have children according to their vocation. Children bring many blessings to the home.

[22] For those couples who are sterile but who wish to have a child, the Church encourages medical research. Such research should always look after the true meaning of the values in marriage discussed earlier: life, love, permanence, self-giving, and deep human fulfillment. We should remember that a child is not property, something to be "owned" or something someone "owes us." Being unable to have children is not evil and may lead to much good. It often leads

couples to adopt children who are otherwise unwanted or to service and charity beyond the norm.

Group or personal process

- How can single people, those in religious life or priesthood, or married people grow to be less unilateral or one-sided and more loving and other-centered?

- Part of being loving toward others, no matter with whom you live, is affirming them. Think about ways in which you can affirm those in your immediate circle. Share these with each other.

- Many Catholic couples regulate the number of children they have, which is in keeping with Catholic teaching and tradition. What are the moral ways they can do that?

PART THREE ✚ **ARTICLES 2380–2391 AND 2514–2527 OF THE *CATECHISM***

Challenges to marriage

[23] From the earliest times, the people of God have taught that adultery is always wrong. It breaks the marriage promise and is selfish and unilateral. Adultery is an injustice because it violates the rights of the other spouse, undermines marriage as an institution, and compromises the good of having children.

[24] The gospels are silent on most matters related to sexuality, but on the question of marriage as lifelong, Jesus seems insistent. Canon law in the Church echoes this rather firm position where, in canon

1141, it says without doubt that between the baptized, marriages cannot be dissolved by anyone or anything short of death. This is true, of course, only if the marriage bond was entered into without impediments and with complete freedom.

[25] Spouses may separate during marriage, and civil divorce can be acceptable to protect certain legal rights, to protect one from violence or abuse, to provide for the proper care of the children, or to protect an inheritance. Under such circumstances, civil divorce may be the best moral choice.

[26] But without such good reasons, divorce works against our life-long journey to holiness and peace. It breaks a contract entered into before God and all; it hurts the spouses and their children; it upsets the common good; and if one spouse is deserted, even more harm is done. In the latter case, the abandoned spouse, of course, is in good moral standing, because he or she has tried to be faithful. In general, civil divorce entered into for any reason outside of those cited above is a grave moral wrong.

[27] Christian men and women have only one spouse because polygamy is seen to throw out of balance the idea that each spouse has equal dignity in the covenant of marriage. Incest corrupts family relationships and suggests an unhealthy sexuality.

[28] The sexual abuse of children or adolescents is scandalous, and the harm done by it usually lasts throughout one's lifetime. It is an unhealthy human behavior and against the civil and moral law.

[29] When a couple lives together without benefit of marriage, sharing sexual intimacy and even having children, they endanger themselves. The lack of long-term commitment to be faithful creates a situation where neither party can be sure that the other is truly and

firmly "there for them." Is this based on a lack of mutual trust? Or is it based on a desire for short-term love? Or is it based on a lack of serious thought? It is certainly not seen as preparation for the commitment of marriage.

The ninth commandment

[30] "You shall not covet your neighbor's wife," we read in Exodus, chapter 20, verse 17. Even though verse 17 goes on to describe other forms of greed, Catholic tradition has considered this phrase to comprise the ninth commandment. We give a name to the intense human desire to have and own what belongs to another; we call it "concupiscence."

WE BELIEVE

Purity of heart enables us to remain close to God. It helps us see the world as God sees it. This demands prayer, honesty, chastity, and commitment on our part.

---

[31] At the time that the Book of Exodus was written, wives were considered to be the property of their husbands. And while this is no longer true in most parts of the world, there remains a dark human inclination to crave and yearn for what we should leave alone. St. Paul urges us, however, to walk by the Spirit if we live by it, to put on Christ like a garment, and to put aside unilateral and one-sided desires in favor of those based in love. Only by doing so will we ever find happiness.

[32] But purifying the heart is a struggle, because once seized by this deep desire, this deep lustful emotional fantasy, we can barely escape its grasp. "Blessed are the pure in heart," Jesus teaches in the

Sermon on the Mount. Blessed are those who attune their hearts to love, who put others above themselves, who practice charity toward others, and who follow the way of God. The pure of heart see the human body with all its potential to excite and pleasure us as a temple of the Holy Spirit.

[33] Sexual urges and excitement are wonderful and holy, but they lead to peace and joy only when they are shared within marriage, and even then, only when they are loving.

[34] Purity requires modesty, and modesty means dressing, talking, thinking, looking, and acting only with moderation. Modesty protects the mystery of persons and their love. It encourages patience and moderation in loving relationships. It avoids the allurements of fashion and of exhibiting ourselves too much. In some cultures modesty is a greater value than in others, but all Christians should practice modesty and teach it to their children. We should shape our media to reduce widespread eroticism and sexual illusion.

[35] In the end, following the sixth and ninth commandments requires of us loving self-discipline and a deep Christian spirituality, choosing love first and dying to ourselves so that we might rise with great joy!

Group or personal process

- In your general, day-to-day exposure to media and advertising, how much of a role does sexual fantasy play in alluring customers? What is your own response to that?

- How can we learn self-discipline and teach it to others?

- How are the "pure of heart" blessed?

Prayer

You have made us for love, O God, and we now commit ourselves to follow the pathway you have set for us. With your divine wisdom, you have implanted within us the desire to form marriages and communities of love. Send your Spirit to us now so that we might tame our selfish desires and turn our hearts toward others, reflecting your own divine heart. We make this prayer through Christ, our Lord. Amen.

Session Six

POSSESSIONS, GREED, & GENEROSITY:
the 7th and 10th commandments

BASED ON ARTICLES 2401–2449 AND 2534–2550 OF THE
CATECHISM OF THE CATHOLIC CHURCH. TO READ A SUMMARY OF THIS
SECTION, SEE *CATECHISM* ARTICLES 2450–2463 AND 2551–2557

Introduction

The seventh commandment calls us to the practice of justice and charity in how we handle and manage earthly goods and the fruits of our labor. The goods of creation are destined for the entire human race. The right to private property does not abolish the universal destination of goods. The dominion granted by the Creator over the mineral, vegetable, and animal resources of the universe cannot be separated from respect for moral obligations, including those toward generations to come. The tenth commandment forbids avarice arising from a passion for riches and their attendant power.

Scripture

READER: A reading from the Gospel of Matthew.

"Do not store up for yourselves treasures on earth, where moth and rust consume and where thieves break in and steal; but store up for yourselves treasures in heaven, where neither moth nor rust consumes and where thieves do not break in and steal. For where your treasure is, there your heart will be also. No one can serve two masters; for a slave will either hate the one and love the other, or be devoted to the one and despise the other. You cannot serve God and wealth." (MATTHEW 6:19–21, 24)

READER: The word of the Lord.

ALL: Thanks be to God.

Possessions, greed, and generosity

[1] "You shall not steal," we read in Exodus, chapter 20, verse 15. We Christians take this to mean that any time we have or take more than our share, any time we act without charity and justice, any time we violate the right to private property, we are living outside the bounds of this commandment.

[2] From the beginning, the earth and its resources have been entrusted to us humans to use and to protect. These resources aren't given to a minority of people but to all—to be shared fairly. Even if we own private land or personal property, we are still bound to take into account the needs of those around us who do not have the means to support themselves and their families. No one may have more than his or her fair share.

[3] We are, in fact, only temporarily entrusted with whatever we have now. It will always remain part of the "global trust" that belongs to all humankind, both now living and yet to be born. Goods of production such as land and factories, skills and talents, are to be used for the benefit of all.

[4] For their part, those who consume such goods must do so in moderation, reserving the larger portion for the sick and poor. Governments have the right and duty to regulate ownership to achieve this goal. We must, in other words, be moderate, just, and oriented to the common good.

WE BELIEVE

The goods of creation are meant to be shared in the entire human family. The right to private property does not release us from the requirement to share generously.

When are we stealing?

[5] Whenever we take something that does not belong to us without the consent of the owner, we are stealing. If the refusal of the owner to give us something is unreasonable and causes harm, we are not stealing if we take it anyway. This is especially true in cases of urgent necessity, such as taking food when we are starving, or using shelter if we have none.

[6] But if we borrow things and keep them, or fail to return found items, or engage in business fraud, or pay unjust wages, or force prices up unfairly or illegally, we are stealing. Also, if we engage in deceit to affect decisions, or take things for private use from a company, or do work poorly on purpose, or evade paying taxes, or forge checks or invoices, or engage in excessive spending and waste, or willfully damage property, we are stealing.

[7] Also, if we break promises and contracts or fail to pay our just debts, or fail to safeguard property under our care, we are stealing. In these cases, we are bound to make restitution, that is, to repaying what we have stolen and making right what we have wronged.

[8] Playing cards and gambling for money is not contrary to this commandment unless the passion for it overtakes us. Unfair wagers, however, and cheating at games constitute serious moral wrongs. Enslaving other people is strictly forbidden by this commandment.

The resources of the earth

[9] The use of the resources of the earth must be based on respect for its integrity. We may not abuse plant life, animal life, or minerals. We may not consume more than the earth itself can reasonably support and replace. No one person or group of persons in a nation may take so much of these resources for themselves that others suffer either now or in generations to come.

Group or personal process

- From what you are reading here, how easy is it for us to be unaware that we have more than we need, or that we are engaged in taking what does not belong to us?

- How can we create a just economic system in which the goods of the earth are shared with all? Why do some have so much more than others?

- Read faith statement #9 again and talk about how we can care for creation more faithfully. What must we give up, do, or stop doing?

The care of the animals

[10] We are bound by this commandment to treat animals with gentleness and care. We are their stewards, and they are not our servants. It's acceptable to use animals for food and clothing. They may be domesticated to help us in our work and recreation. Medical and scientific experimentation on animals is a morally acceptable practice, provided it remains within reasonable limits and contributes to caring for or saving human lives.

[11] Our sense of human dignity leads us to teach that we should never cause animals to suffer or die needlessly. It is likewise uncharitable to spend money on them that should go to the relief of human misery. We can love our animals, but we should not direct to them the affection due only to persons, as article 2418 of the *Catechism* reminds us.

Catholic social teaching

[12] We believe that the gospel reveals to us how men and women should live together. The pastors of the Church make judgments, therefore, about economic and social matters when fundamental human rights or the care of our spirituality demands it. The teachings of the Church on this are living. From time to time they grow and develop, as they have been doing since the nineteenth century at the dawn of industrial society.

[13] As times change, the Church clarifies its teaching in the light of the Holy Spirit. We teach, therefore, that economic factors are not the basis on which the human family is based. Profit is not the exclusive measure of social progress, nor is profit the be-all and end-

all of economic activity. The measure and goal of economic activity is the human family: its security, comfort, and good will.

[14] So even if it doesn't make economic sense according to the latest economic theories, the goods of the earth must reach every person in accordance with justice and charity. Failing to achieve this will result in war and terrorism as people struggle to obtain their due.

[15] The pastors of the Church have "rejected the totalitarian and atheistic ideologies associated in modem times with 'communism' or 'socialism'" (*Catechism*, article 2425). But they have also rejected the form of capitalism that places profits over human good. The pastors of the Church support reasonable regulation of the marketplace to protect workers and distribute goods justly.

WE BELIEVE
The goal of all economic activity must be the care and fulfillment of each human being; we cannot make pure profit our goal. Everyone must be given the chance to work.

---

[16] Working is everyone's right and duty and brings human dignity. When we work we fulfill our human destiny, the potential inscribed in us by God. Each worker should be able to earn enough to live on in wages, benefits, or other goods. Every person has the right to start a business and to use his or her talents for gain. Business owners, their employees, and government should work together to negotiate compensation.

[17] Governments should also provide for the freedoms, stable currencies, rights to private property, and efficient public utilities and services that make business possible. Governments should also

make sure human rights are honored in every business, but business owners are primarily responsible for this. Each worker must be provided a chance to work, and professions must be open to all without discrimination based on gender, health, or nationality. Just wages are required, of course, and workers may strike if they are not paid, provided there is no violence.

[18] On the international level in today's world are some rich nations and many poor ones. This inequality is based on greed, the arms race, and unfair financial systems. Rich nations have a grave moral responsibility toward those which are poor to help them develop an economic system that can provide for their people.

[19] And in the meantime, rich nations must, in charity, provide immediate relief to the poor, especially during catastrophes and epidemics. The efforts of poor countries working for growth and liberation must be supported. The pastors of the Church should not intervene in the business affairs of nations, but lay Catholics should apply their faith and lead their nations in charity.

Group or personal process

- Who is rich today? Compare your own wealth to that of the average person in the world? How do you compare?

- Read faith statements #18–19 again. How does this teaching challenge us Christians to have a greater heart for the poor but also to get to work to end or reduce poverty? What can we do to accomplish this goal?

Loving the poor

[20] Having a heart for the materially poor has long been a part of Christian life. The poor were also at the heart of Jesus' teaching—and often they were the first to receive him. In fact, in the Gospel of Matthew, chapter 25, love for the poor becomes the test by which we are found worthy to enter the kingdom of God.

[21] For the rich, this is a difficult teaching and one that is often overlooked. Anyone who has more than he or she needs for their basic needs and for those wants that bring human dignity, such as education and health care, or retirement in old age, is stealing the rest from the poor. That which is due in justice to the poor should not be offered as a gift of charity. When we attend to the poor and share our goods with them, we are giving them *what is theirs, not ours,* as article 2446 of the *Catechism* reminds us.

Works of mercy

[22] We are called to perform spiritual works of mercy, such as instructing, advising, consoling, comforting, forgiving, and bearing wrongs patiently. We are also called to perform corporal works of mercy, such as feeding the hungry and sheltering the homeless, clothing the naked and visiting the sick and imprisoned.

The tenth commandment

[23] "You shall not covet your neighbor's house," we read in Exodus, chapter 20, verse 17. "You shall not covet your neighbor's...male or female slave, or ox or donkey, or anything that belongs to your neighbor." The tenth commandment shifts the focus of yearning for what is not our own to the heart.

[24] We humans have appetites: strong urges to eat when we're hungry, to be warm when we're cold, and to taste this or that food or drink. By themselves these appetites are natural and fine, but they can lead us to excess or to desire what is not ours to have. The tenth commandment forbids greed and the desire to amass earthly goods without limit.

[25] If we have an inordinate passion for riches and the power that comes with them, we are out of the bounds of this commandment. If we're a merchant who desires scarcity to drive up prices, a doctor who wants people to get sick, or a lawyer who wants people to have troubles, we're out of bounds.

WE BELIEVE

This commandment teaches us to avoid greed and envy by following Jesus more closely, by loving the poor as our sisters and brothers, and by practicing the art of self-giving love.

---

[26] This commandment urges us to detect envy when it arises within our hearts. Envy often leads to hatred, gossip, joy when others have misfortune, or displeasure when someone else does well. But we Christians learn from Jesus, our teacher, to rejoice in the success of others and to celebrate when they are happy. We cooperate with grace, and we practice the ways of the Spirit, which are good will and humility.

[27] The Church reminds us that Jesus taught us to be more detached from riches in order to enter into the kingdom of God. "Blessed are the poor in spirit," we read in Matthew, chapter 5. If we want to be happy, in other words, we must seek consolation in spiritual things, not in material ones.

[28] In the end, the deep human desire to be happy that leads us always to God frees us from being too attached to material things. In fact, true happiness and even true wealth come only when we give away what we have without seeking praise or attention. When we empty ourselves and our pocketbooks, we gain fullness of life through Christ. When we die to ourselves financially, when we develop a heart for the poor, and when we trust only in God to save us, we find the peace we seek.

Group or personal process

- Why is it so difficult for people to part with their money and property?

- When we are self-giving in love, we let go of even those things that we hold most dear; we learn the art of detachment from things and attachment to love. What are you called to bring into this? From what are you called to detach?

- What causes us to yearn for more possessions and power? Why do we always seem to want just one more thing to add to our "pile of stuff"?

Prayer

We seek you with a sincere heart, O God, and we yearn to cleanse our hearts of all that keeps us away from you. Now we pray for the grace to be detached from possessions and money so that our hearts will have room in them for you. We pray that the poor and disenfranchised of society may also find a place within our hearts and our wallets. May your Spirit stir up within us the desire to share what we have and care for all the peoples of the earth. We make this prayer through Christ, our Lord. Amen.

Session Seven

HONESTY: *the 8ᵗʰ commandment*

BASED ON ARTICLES 2464–2503 OF THE *CATECHISM OF THE CATHOLIC CHURCH*. TO READ A SUMMARY OF THIS SECTION, SEE *CATECHISM* ARTICLES 2504–2513

Introduction

Truthfulness is the virtue that consists in showing oneself true in deeds and truthful in words. Respect for the reputation and honor of persons forbids all gossip and speaking badly of others, even if it is a true statement. Lying consists in saying what is false with the intention of deceiving one's neighbor. The sacramental seal is inviolable. Professional secrets must be kept. Confidences prejudicial to another are not to be divulged.

Scripture

READER: A reading from the Gospel of Matthew.

"Again, you have heard that it was said to those of ancient times, 'You shall not swear falsely, but carry out the vows you have made to the Lord.' But I say to you, do not swear at all, either by heaven, for it is the throne of God, or by the earth, for it is his footstool, or by Jerusalem, for it is the city of the great King. And do not swear by your head, for you cannot make one hair white or black. Let your word be 'Yes, Yes' or 'No, No'; anything more than this comes from the evil one." (MATTHEW 5:33–37)

READER: The word of the Lord.

ALL: Thanks be to God.

PART ONE + **ARTICLES 2464–2474 OF THE** *CATECHISM*
Open, honest, loving, & kind

[1] "You shall not bear false witness against your neighbor," we read in Exodus, chapter 20, verse 16. We are called by this commandment to the truth, to represent it as accurately as possible in both word and deed. Our relationships in life depend upon our doing this—as does the common good.

[2] The basis of this commandment is found in God, whose word is truth, whose law is truth, and who is, indeed, the one true God. Jesus Christ himself was said to be full of truth so that whoever would believe in Christ would not remain in darkness. Deeds and words done in darkness hide truth, but Jesus made this promise in the Gospel of John, chapter 8, to those who had believed in him: "If you continue in my word, you are truly my disciples; and you will know the truth, and the truth will make you free."

[3] Indeed, Jesus later sent the Spirit of Truth as our guide and helper to live within our hearts and teach us.

[4] We believe that we humans, by nature, tend toward living in truth. We also have a moral obligation to tell the truth and to adhere to it once it is understood. That is, we must be true in deeds and truthful in words at all times. We must be sincere and candid about what we know to be true, but we must also be loving and kind in how we express it.

[5] This means we must avoid and guard against deception about the truth; we must avoid gossip, even if what we say is true; we must avoid disguising what is true to make it appear to be something else; and we must avoid insincerity in our relationships with others. We must have confidence in one another that what we hear from each other is true. But not everything that is true must be stated; some things may be kept secret using discretion and charity, especially the secrets of others.

WE BELIEVE

Truth is the virtue by which we show ourselves true in deed and word, guarding against duplicity, half-truths, and hypocrisy.

---

[6] In the First Letter of John we are reminded of the Christian life. "God is light," we read in chapter 1, verses 5 and 6, "and in him there is no darkness at all. If we say that we have fellowship with [God] while we are walking in darkness, we lie and do not do what is true."

To what are we called?

[7] When we are called to speak in public about what we believe, we Christians are bound to tell the truth. Indeed, when Christ was at his trial he told Pilate that he had come into the world to "bear witness to the truth." We who follow him now can do no less.

[8] Many Christians over the centuries have accepted death as martyrs rather than bear false witness to their faith. The term "martyr" today has taken on new meanings, including the suggestion that doing violence to others in the name of Christ, or Allah, or Yahweh, makes one a martyr. But to us Christians, it means simply standing up for truth, refusing to renounce our faith, and accepting whatever fate results from that.

[9] This may mean, for example, refusing to take part in what your peers are doing such as loafing when you should be working, cheating when you should study, drinking too much when moderation is better, or stealing from the office because—and this is the common excuse—"everyone else is doing it."

[10] Standing up for your faith does not mean getting up on a soap box and preaching to the crowds as much as honoring what you know to be right even if only one other person sees you or if no one else sees you. It means following the Way of Christ: be open, honest, loving, and kind; be forgiving even of your enemies; and be generous and hospitable even when it is difficult to be. The term "martyr" means, literally, "witness," and we witness to our faith by living it fully and completely every day.

Group or personal process

- How do we know what is really true? What sources of information can you trust?

- How are you called to witness to your faith, or in other words, to be a martyr?

- In what situations in your society is truth compromised or ignored?

- When is it most difficult for you to tell the truth?

Untruth

[11] In the letter to the Christians at Ephesus, the writer gives us a clear picture in chapter 4, verse 25, of what the early Church expected from believers: "So then, putting away falsehood, let all of us speak the truth to our neighbors, for we are members of one another."

[12] When we lie in court, we are giving what is called "false witness," and when we lie under oath, we are committing what is called "perjury." Both undermine the common good and hurt the innocent. They may also help the guilty go free, and they are both seriously wrong.

[13] Rash judgment occurs when we assume that something about someone else is true even if there is scant evidence to support it. We are called, in fact, to be ready to give others the benefit of the doubt on everything we hear about them. We should outdo one another in charity.

[14] Detraction occurs when we make a derogatory comment about someone else to people who aren't aware of the facts. Calumny occurs when we say things about others that we know to be untrue in order to harm their reputation. In general, this kind of gossip is done to build up the poor self-image of the talker, so we should be slow to engage in this, and we should call others to charity.

[15] Excessive flattery occurs when we praise others even when we know what they have done is wrong or when we know they have behaved falsely. In general we do this in order to ingratiate ourselves with others and to be agreeable or make them seem like friends—but what kind of friend fails to be honest?

[16] Boasting and bragging occur when we exaggerate accomplishments or events in order to seem better than we are. Or when we simply call attention to ourselves for deeds that would better be anonymous.

WE BELIEVE

The golden rule helps us sort out whether in a given situation it is appropriate to reveal the truth to someone who asks for it.

---

[17] Lying is the most direct offense against the truth. When someone has the right to know the truth and, either by speech, action, or even by silence, we lead them to believe something else, we are guilty of deception. Such behavior undermines the very basis of the common good and our relationships with our neighbors. If such deception and lying does serious harm, then the offense is serious, especially if the consequences are deadly. Lying is a failure of both justice and charity.

[18] Lies do real violence to others, affecting people's true judgments and undermining trust. When we are guilty of lying, we must make reparation. That is, we must seek forgiveness and undo as much of the harm as possible, especially if our lie has hurt someone's reputation. We must then amend our lives and commit ourselves to truth telling and honesty.

The truth

[19] The command to tell the truth does not imply that we should repeat every item of news we hear or observe. Sometimes, in charity, we should not speak at all. It's not enough to be open and honest unless we are also loving and kind. We must consider the good and

safety of others and their own right to privacy; it is our duty to avoid scandal. We are never bound to reveal the truth to anyone who does not have the right to know it.

[20] And, of course, the secrets shared in the sacrament of reconciliation are sacred and may never be shared or implied at any time. Confidential information in professional life has a similar level of secrecy attached to it. However, in cases where divulging the truth is necessary for the welfare of those affected, we are bound to do so. For example, if we know by our professional work that someone is being hurt, or that a child is being abused, we must reveal this to proper authorities.

[21] On the whole, we must honor each other's privacy and balance the need for the public to know things with people's dignity and right to keep secrets. This includes workers in the media who may be tempted to reveal to the public details about someone's life for profit.

Group or personal process

- When is it right to withhold the truth, and when it is right to report what we know to be true? Is it ever acceptable to lie?

- There are times when we should simply remain silent about what we know. When are those?

- There are other times when we are bound to speak up about what we have seen and heard. When are those?

The media

[22] We live today in a communications explosion! The average person living today receives in one day's metropolitan newspaper more information than someone in the seventeenth century received in their entire lifetime! And with the advent of the Internet, more and more of the information we receive has questionable or unknown sources. What can we trust?

[23] And what's more, all this media and information today plays a major role in forming public opinion and shaping the culture. The principle to be followed regarding media is this: All public media are at the service of the common good. Society has a right to the truth and—within the limits we have been discussing, those regarding charity and justice—to the *whole* truth.

[24] Social solidarity is a great Christian value, and it is established by shared common knowledge. Ideas must circulate freely, and people must have the right to express themselves even if what they say is contrary to the government. Part of the responsibility for honesty in media rests with the users. Users can tend to become passive, accepting whatever is reported without ever questioning sources or facts. And part of the responsibility for this rests with journalists. Without ever stooping to gossip and defamation, they should report the truth and respect people's right to privacy.

[25] And part of the responsibility for this rests with public authorities. In the first place, they should conduct themselves and the business of government with openness and honesty. Second, they should enact laws that protect freedom of speech and the free flow of information. Third, they should report what they are doing on a regular and public basis and not attempt to manipulate public opin-

ion with half-truths, inferences, and "disinformation." All forms of government that suppress information or punish people for their thoughts, or manipulate witnesses and trials, are seriously wrong.

WE BELIEVE

Society has a right to know the truth, to live in freedom, and to be offered justice in all economic and political matters.

Truth, beauty, and art

[26] Sometimes truth is so sublime and wonderful that we are rendered "speechless." There are no words to express the depth or heights of what we know to be true. Love is like this. How do you express love? The depths of the human heart are wordless, as are the exaltations of our spiritual lives or the mystery of God. We humans also express our truths in forms other than words or deeds. One of these forms is artistic expression.

[27] When you think about it, you realize that art is distinctively human. Animals and plants, beautiful though they are, do not engage in art: painting or sketching, theater or song writing, poetry or sculpture, among other forms. And, similar to the search for the necessities of life, art is universal in the human family.

[28] We speak with the language of art when ordinary words fail us. Liturgical ritual is actually a form of such art: candles, incense, sacred books and vessels, processions and gestures and scripts: it is the "theater of the holy." Art gives expression to deep-seated emotions within us. It is transcendent, mysterious, and spiritual. Sacred art has a special role in prayer, but all art that expresses truth is sacred. For this reason, pastors and bishops should promote and honor true art—old and new—in all its forms.

Group or personal process

- How can we ensure that media, government, and the arts truly reflect the real truth?

- How do you know what is true when you hear or read the news? Whom do you trust to deliver the truth in every situation?

Prayer

O God, you made us and you know us. You know what is deep within our hearts. Send your Spirit to us now, the Spirit of truth and kindness, of openness and honesty. May we always act with the dignity you have given us as human beings. May we treat one another with the same charity with which we hope to be treated ourselves. And may your truth reside in our hearts, now and forever. Amen.